My coloring book Of Animals

This book belong to:

....

....

ZZZ

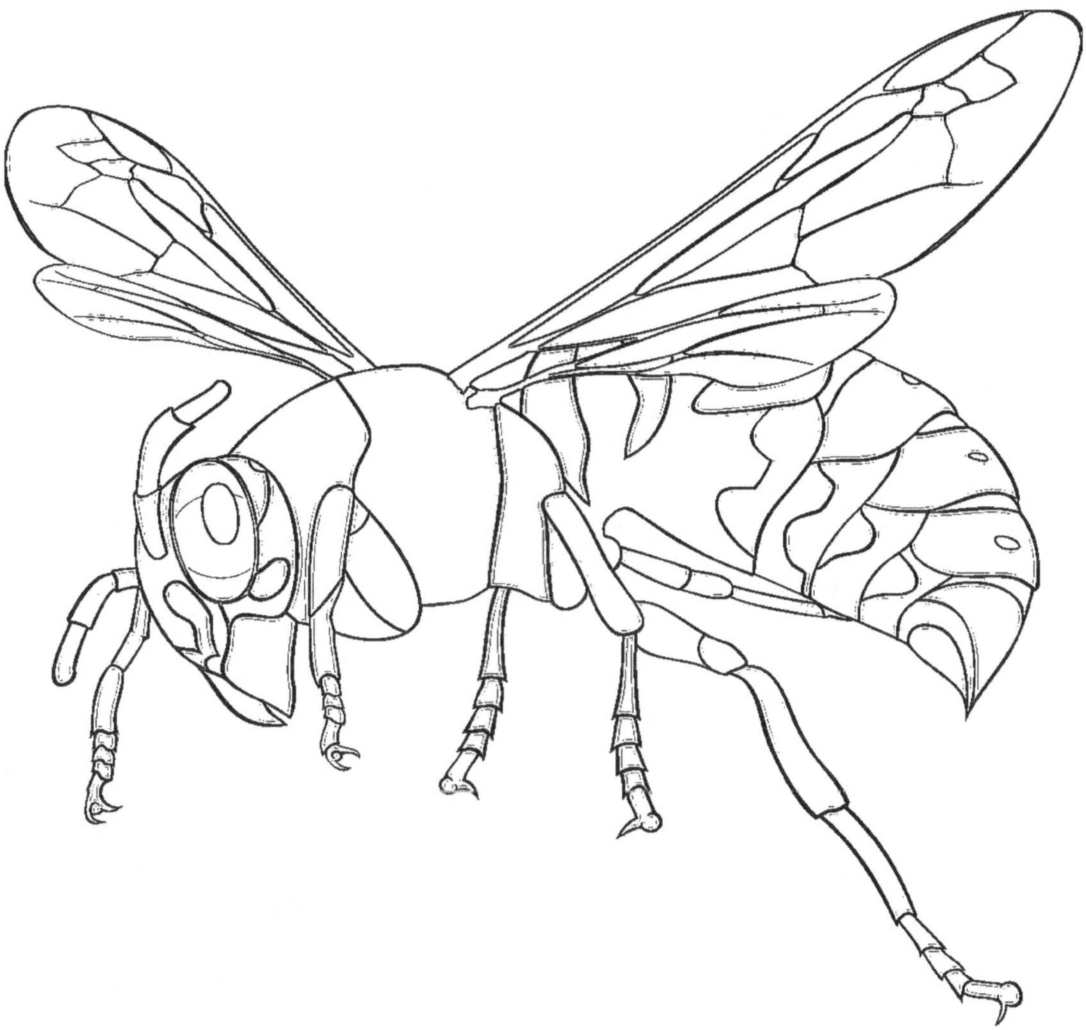

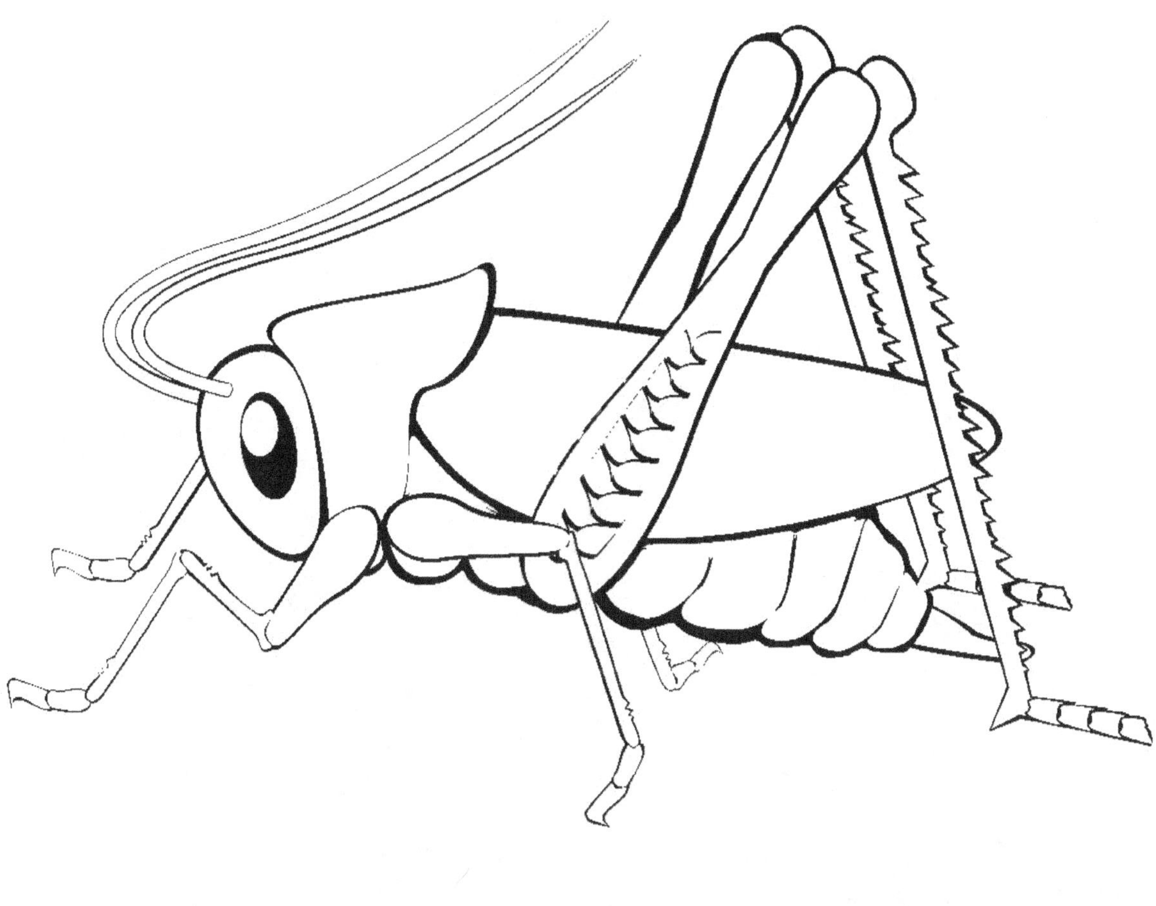

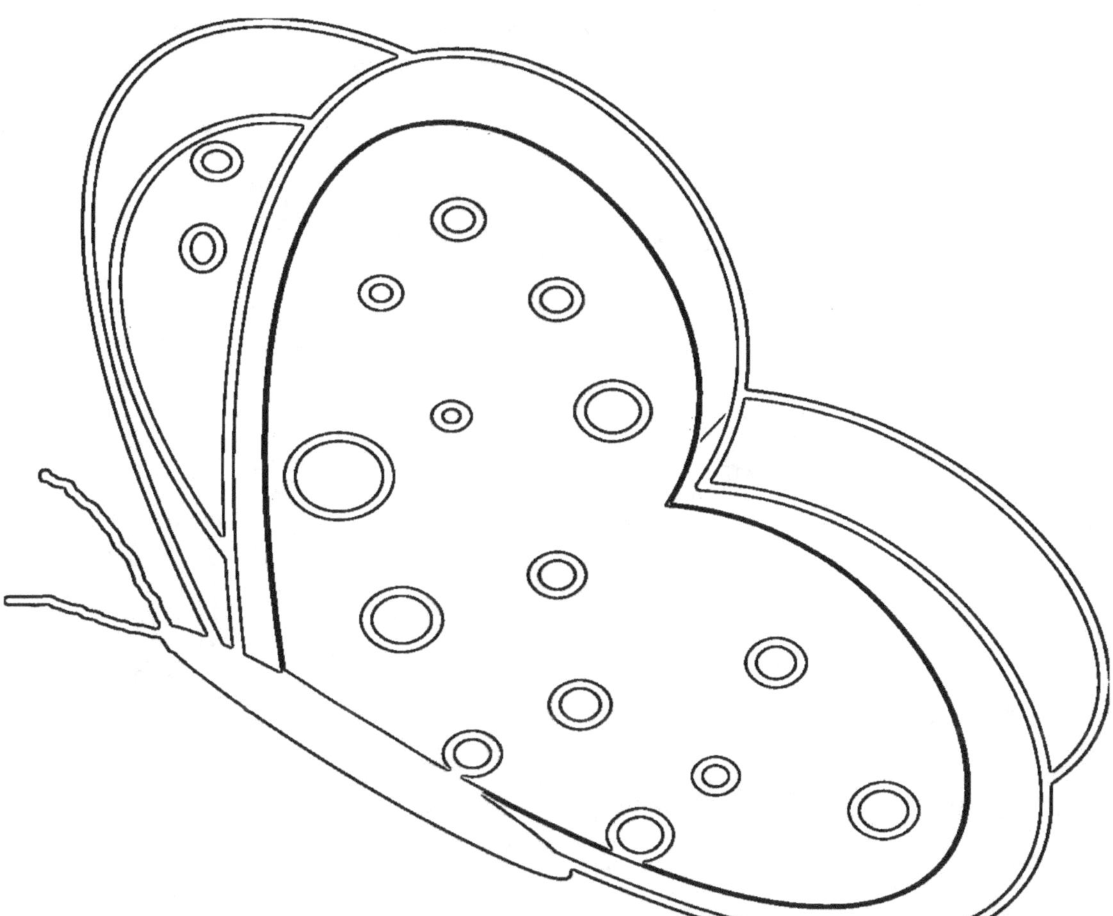

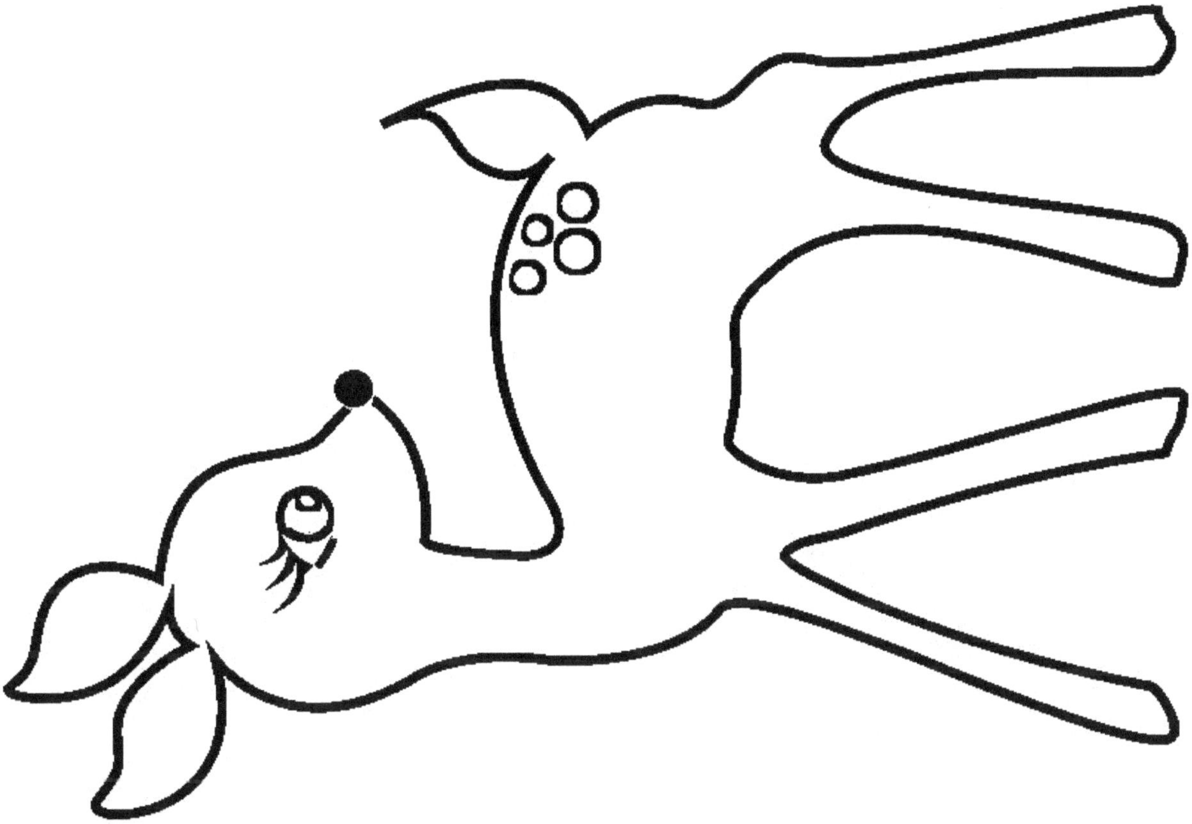

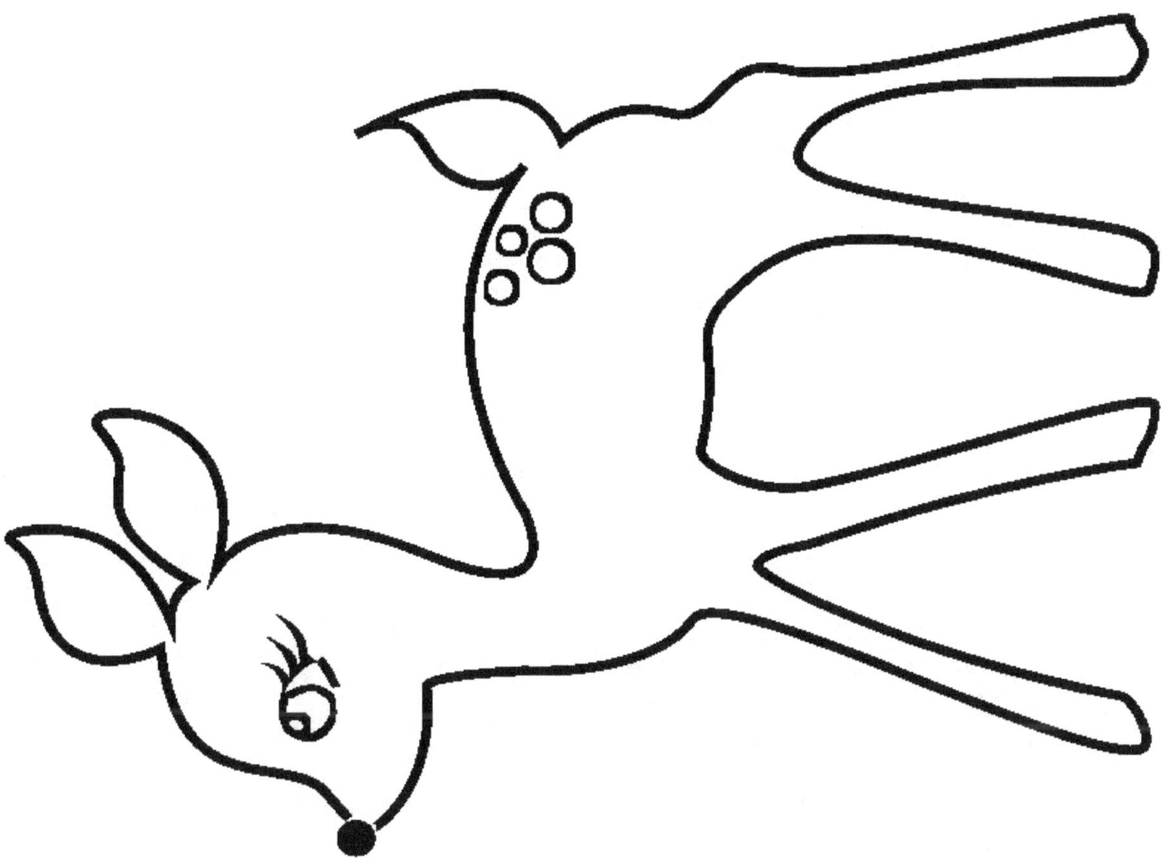

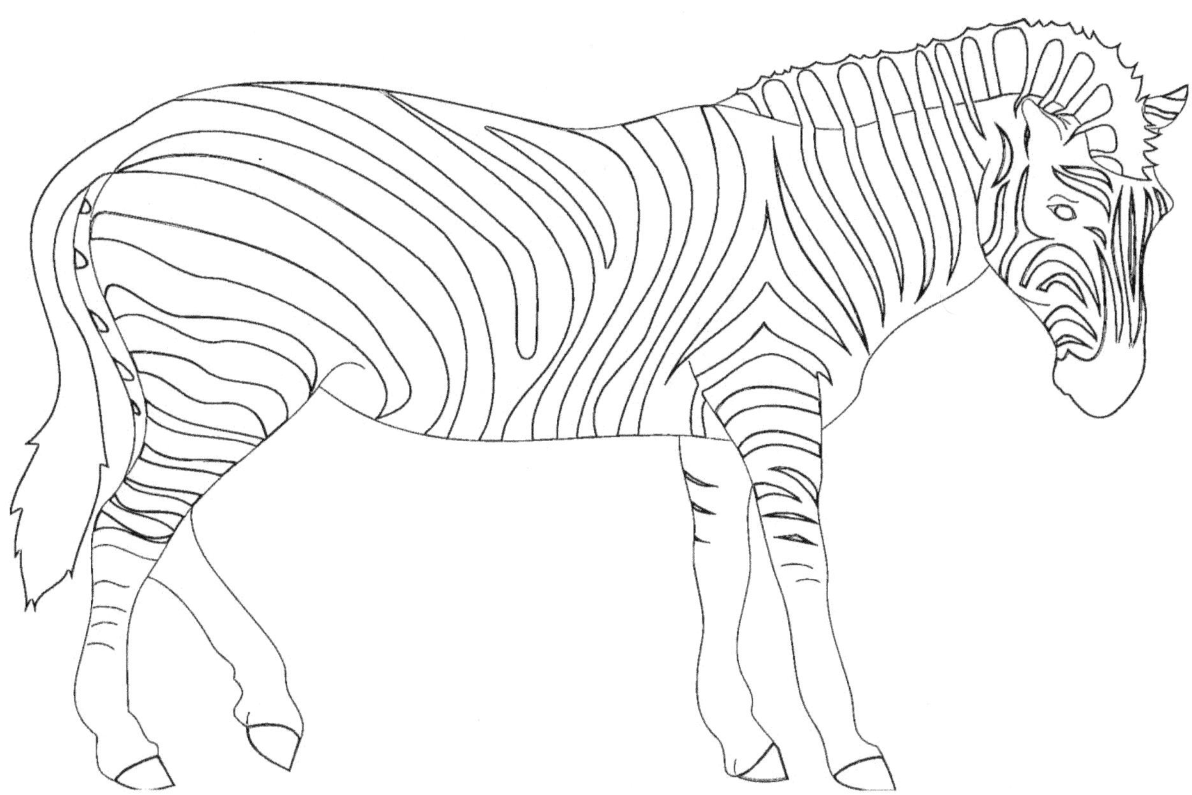

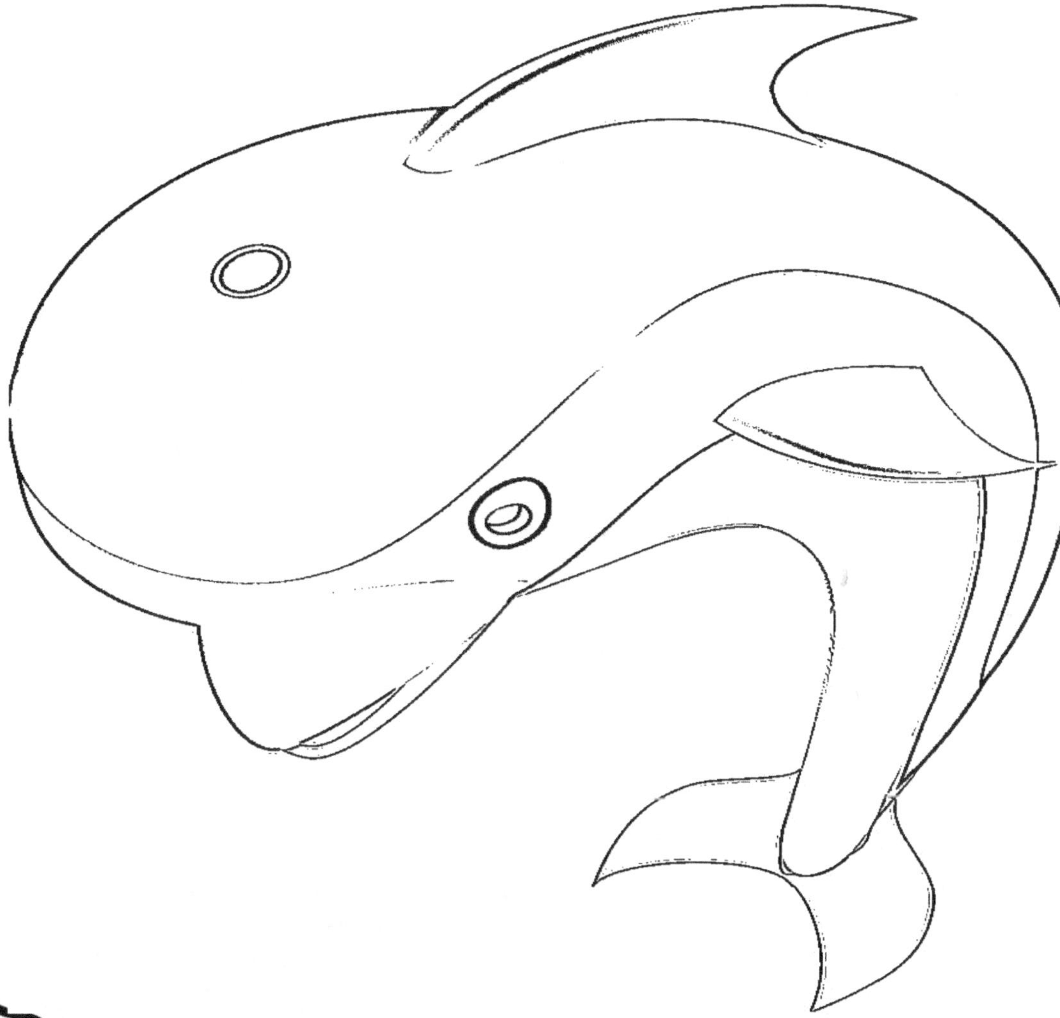

COFFEE
LOVER

www.ingramcontent.com/pod-product-compliance
Lightning Source LLC
Chambersburg PA
CBHW081439250726
48662CB00009B/2872
9798593155122